On the Backs of the Enslaved

On the Backs of the Enslaved
Copyright © 2019 CherylAnne Amendola

Children's Book, Nonfiction, United States History, Biography

All rights reserved. No part of this book may be reproduced in any manner whatsoever, or stored in any information storage system, without the prior written consent of the publisher or the author, except in the case of brief quotations with proper reference, embodied in critical articles and reviews.

Image Credits:
Front cover image and all story illustrations by Allison O'Donnell

Story Text Copyright © CherylAnne Amendola
www.teachinghistoryherway.com

ISBN: 9781704007328
Imprint: Independently published
Amazon Kindle Direct Publishing

Thomas Jefferson was one of the most accomplished men in American history. Along with representing our country in France, he was Secretary of State and even became the third president of the United States.

But like all great people, Thomas did many things that weren't so great at all.

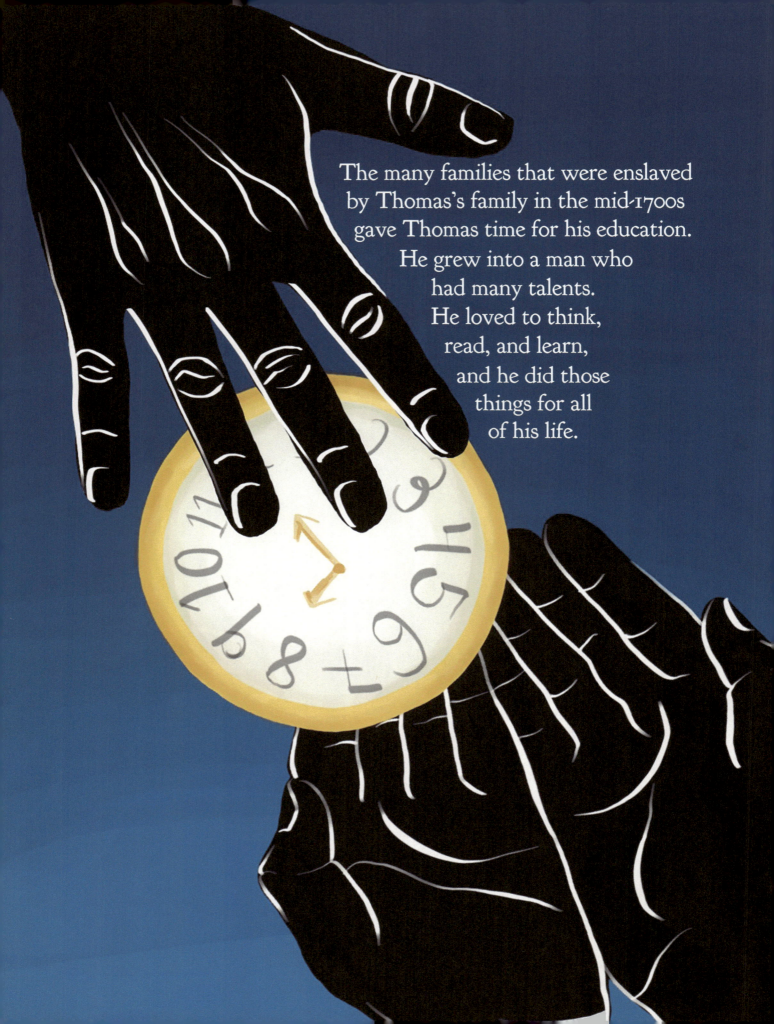

The many families that were enslaved by Thomas's family in the mid-1700s gave Thomas time for his education. He grew into a man who had many talents. He loved to think, read, and learn, and he did those things for all of his life.

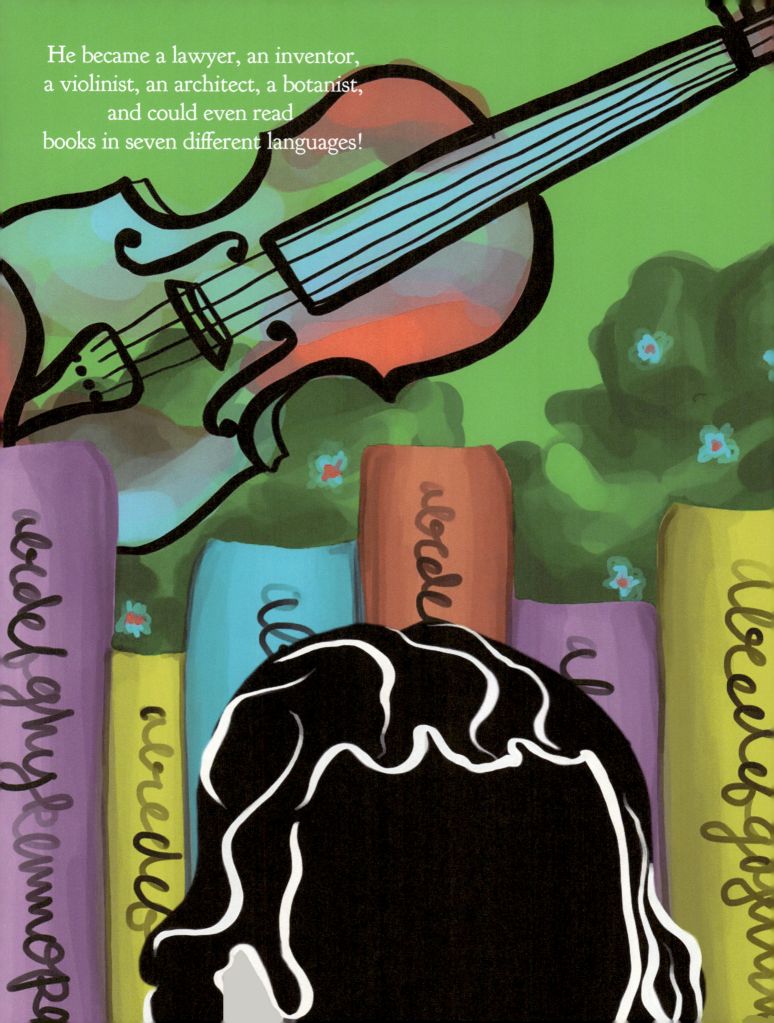

He became a lawyer, an inventor, a violinist, an architect, a botanist, and could even read books in seven different languages!

Thomas used his talents to help the United States become a new country. Up until 1776, the United States was controlled by Great Britain. The American people wanted to be in charge of their own government because they thought Great Britain and their king treated them unfairly.

Life Liberty and happiness

In the Declaration, Thomas wrote that he thought that all people should be free to have "life, liberty, and the pursuit of happiness." It was here that he also wrote, "All men are created equal."

During his life, Thomas enslaved over six hundred black people at his home called Monticello.

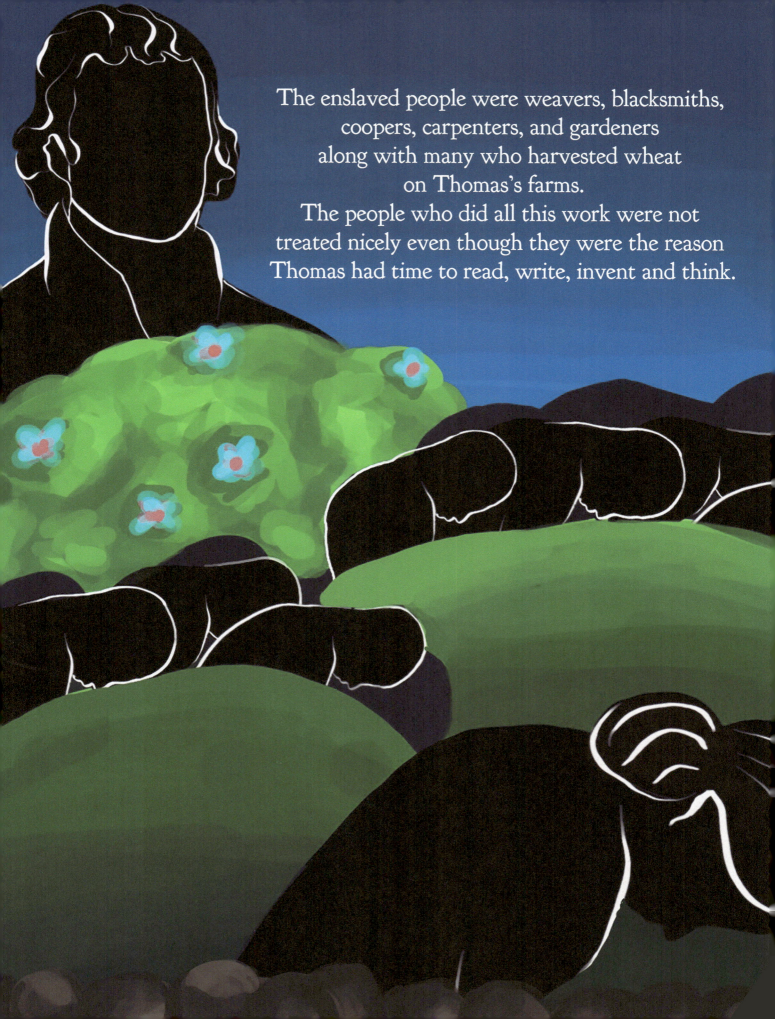

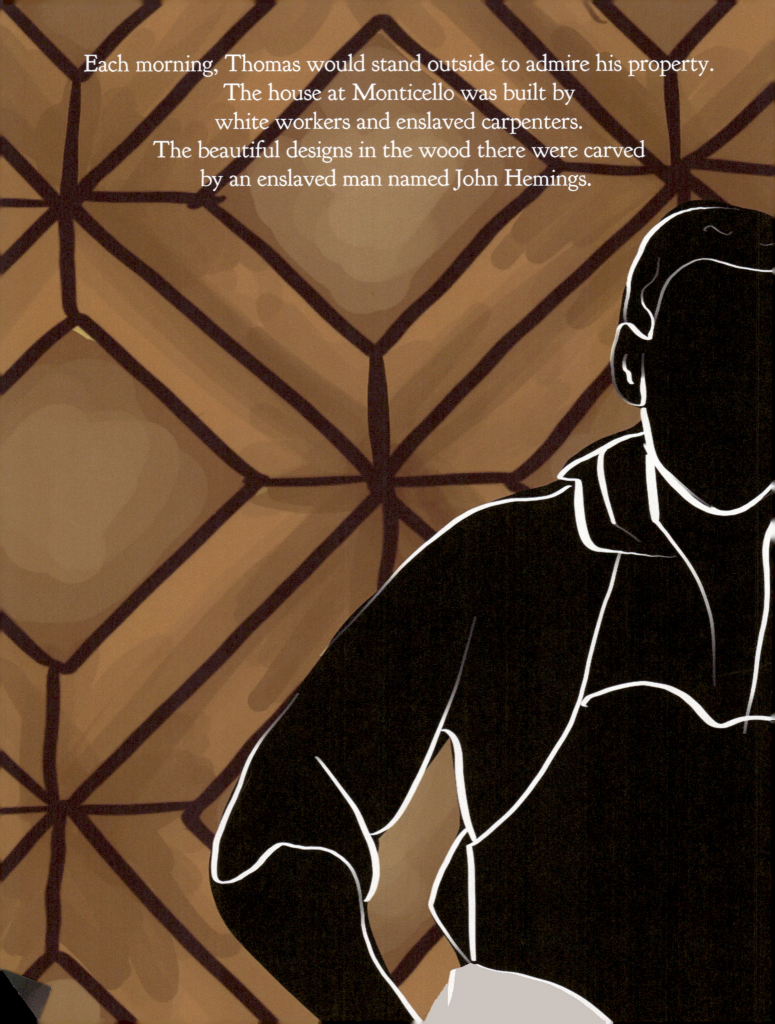

Each morning, Thomas would stand outside to admire his property. The house at Monticello was built by white workers and enslaved carpenters. The beautiful designs in the wood there were carved by an enslaved man named John Hemings.

John and the other people enslaved by Thomas lived in other places near Thomas's house at Monticello. The people who worked in Thomas's wheat fields lived in cabins near where they worked. Some lived in rooms in Thomas's basement. Those who were house servants lived in small log houses very near to Thomas's big house on a street called Mulberry Row.

When they turned ten, boys went to work making nails and girls weaved fabric. If they were good at these jobs, they learned a trade when they turned sixteen. If they were not good at making nails or weaving, they were sent to work in the fields, which was very, very hard.

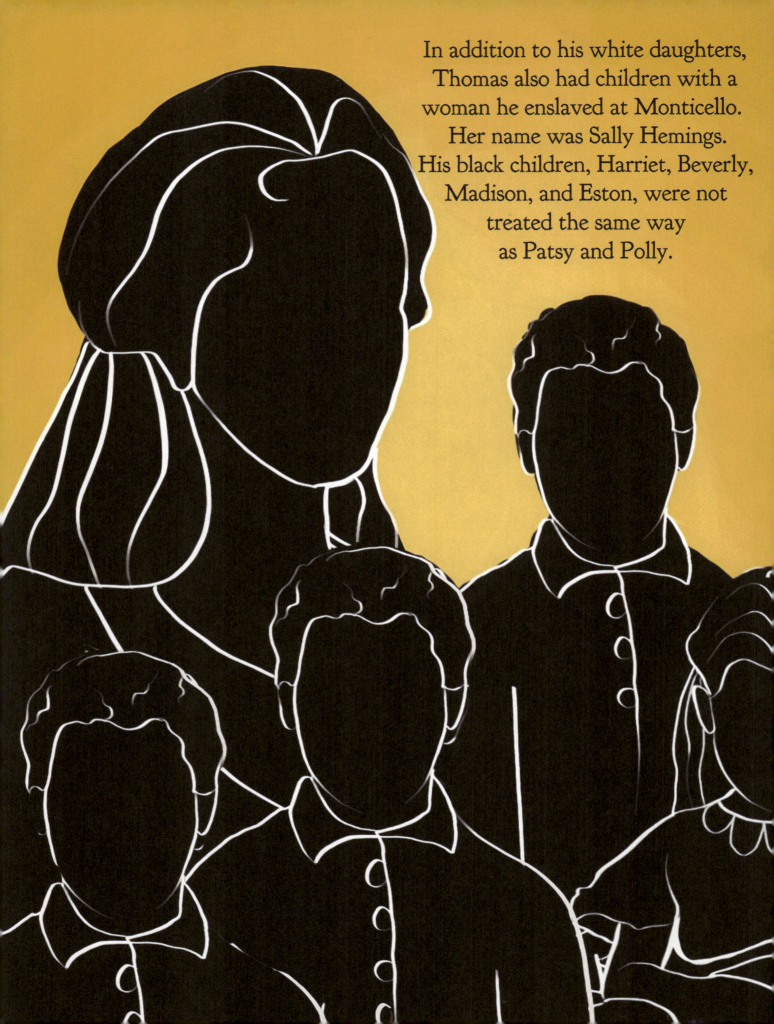

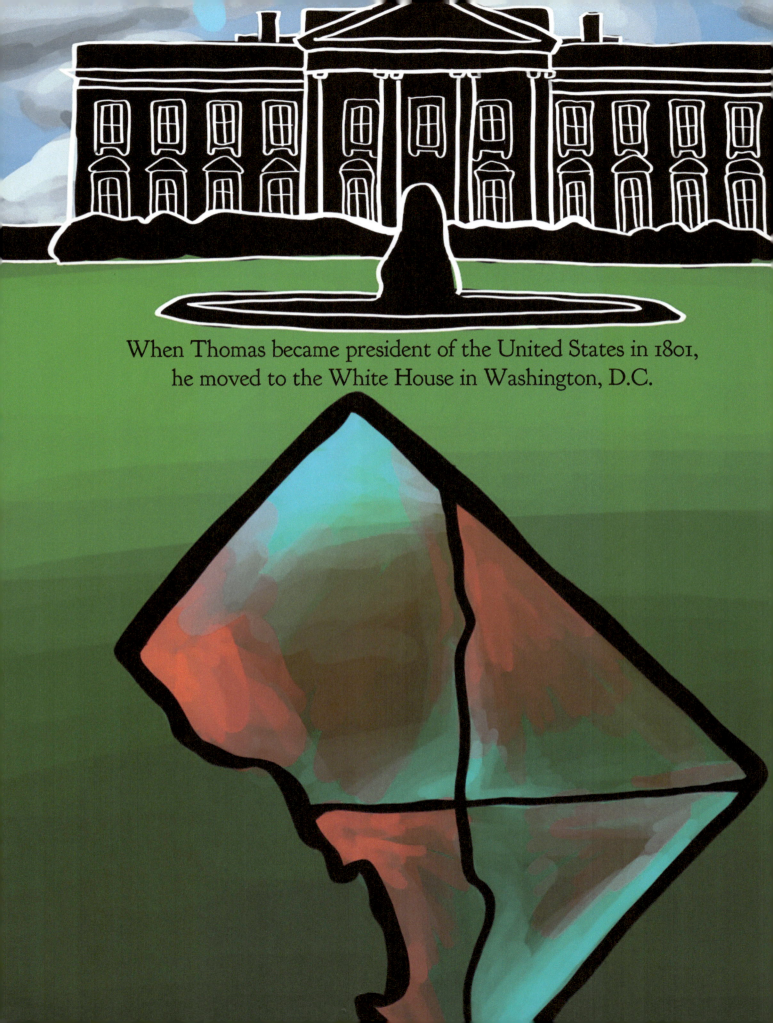

When Thomas became president of the United States in 1801, he moved to the White House in Washington, D.C.

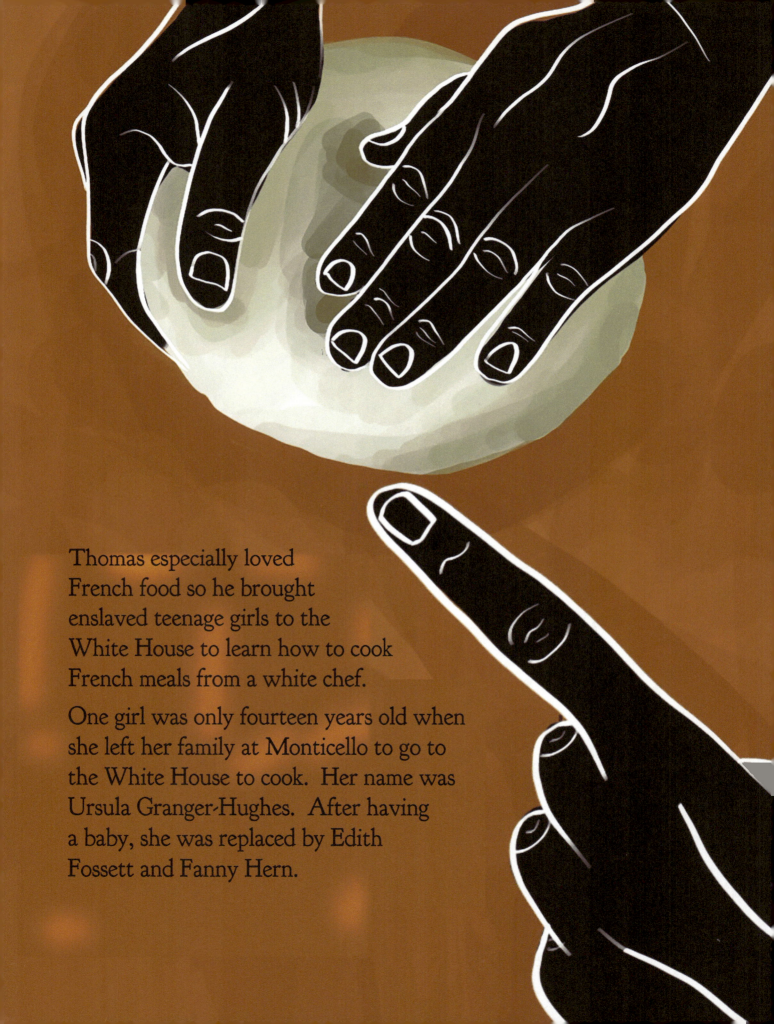

Thomas especially loved French food so he brought enslaved teenage girls to the White House to learn how to cook French meals from a white chef.

One girl was only fourteen years old when she left her family at Monticello to go to the White House to cook. Her name was Ursula Granger-Hughes. After having a baby, she was replaced by Edith Fossett and Fanny Hern.

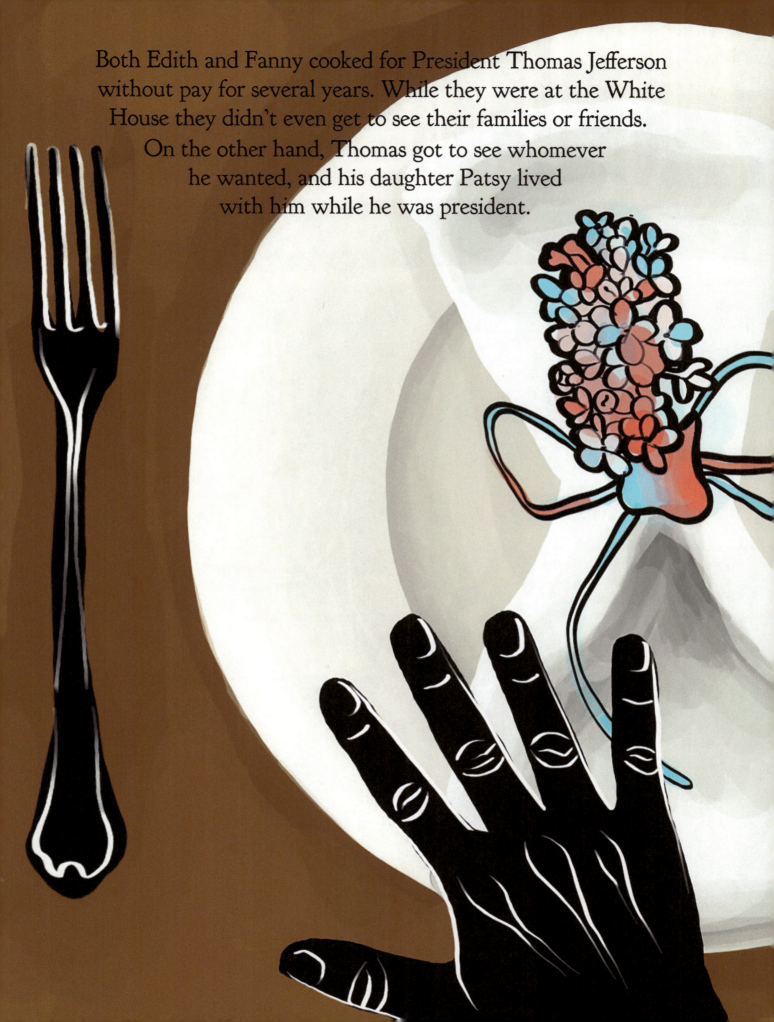

Both Edith and Fanny cooked for President Thomas Jefferson without pay for several years. While they were at the White House they didn't even get to see their families or friends. On the other hand, Thomas got to see whomever he wanted, and his daughter Patsy lived with him while he was president.

During his life at Monticello, he designed automatic doors, a clock that could also show what day it was, and used a simple machine to make copies of his writing.

He also spent plenty of time in his garden experimenting with different kinds of plants. His favorites were peas
—he grew 15 varieties—
and figs.

One of Thomas's proudest achievements, after he retired, was planning and opening the University of Virginia. He designed the buildings and decided what students would learn.

When the university first opened,
only white male students were allowed to attend.

White only

The people who constructed the beautiful buildings
were enslaved African Americans,
and they were not welcome inside to learn.

When Thomas died on July 4, 1826, he freed two of the enslaved children he fathered, Madison and Eston, and a few men: Joseph Fossett, John Hemings, and Burwell Colbert.

He did not free anyone else and they were sold at a slave auction right on Thomas's front lawn.

Some, like Joseph, tried to buy their own wives and children so that they no longer had to be enslaved. Many were separated from their families, and the auction at Monticello was the last time they saw one another.

In the end, it was enslaved people who allowed for
Thomas to pursue his dreams,
and even though he did not live by his own words,
he left us with one of the greatest expressions ever written.

"All men are created equal" means
that everyone should be able
to play and learn,
choose their own work,
and love who their hearts tell them to.

While Thomas Jefferson did not live by his own words,
he gave us an idea to work for:
equality for all to pursue their own happiness.

all men are equal.

About the Author:

CherylAnne Amendola has been teaching American and World History since 2006. She graduated from Teachers College, Columbia University with an M.A. in Social Studies Education. She believes all people's histories should be represented in the classroom. Visit her at: http://www.teachinghistoryherway.com

For RMA. With love, Mommy

About the Illustrator:

Allison Grace O'Donnell is a sophmore studying studio art and legal studies in Washington D.C. She is most passionate about the intersection between creative expression and social justice.

Thank you for pushing me, Cuneo. You will be missed. -A.G.O

All research for this book was conducted at Thomas Jefferson's Monticello and at www.monticello.org.

CPSIA information can be obtained
at www.ICGtesting.com
Printed in the USA
BVHW021349051119
562972BV00009B/38/P